How to be an Ancient Egyptian in 13 easy stages

Contents

Written and illustrated by Scoular Anderson

Collins

Get on the river

The country of Egypt lies at the eastern end of the Mediterranean sea. The people called the Ancient Egyptians lived in this land 5,000 years ago. The river Nile is the longest river in the world and flows through the middle of Egypt.

a rich woman going on a business trip

a farmer moving some cows

2

Most of the land in Egypt was dry desert and rocky hills. Few Ancient Egyptians went into the desert – they thought it was a dangerous and scary place. Instead, they lived near the river Nile. The water of the Nile made the river banks green with trees, bushes and flowers. Farmers could grow crops in the rich, damp soil.

There were no roads. If you were an Ancient Egyptian you used the river to travel up and down the country. The Nile was busy with all sorts of boats.

a big ship carrying heavy cargo like sacks of grain or blocks of stone

Fishermen made boats of reeds. The reeds were bound tightly together with rope.

Sow some seeds

It didn't rain much in Egypt.
For many months the land was
dry and dusty, but once a year
there was heavy rain far away
to the south. The rain made
the water rise in the river Nile.
It flooded the land and made
the ground wet and good for
growing things.

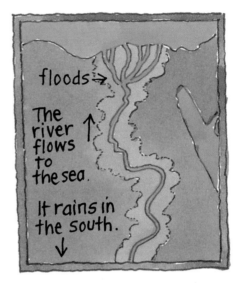

floods →

The
river
flows
to
the sea.

It rains in
the south.
↓

If you were an Ancient Egyptian farmer you leapt into
action when this happened. You ploughed your fields
and sowed corn and vegetable seeds. You trapped water
in **canals** to pour on your crops.

ploughing
↓

sowing seeds
↙

water from a canal
to water the crops
↓

canal

A shaduf was like a crane
← for lifting water.

4

When the corn
in the fields was
ripe, it was cut down
with a sickle.

A sickle was
a wooden tool
with a sharp
stone blade.

The corn grains were
knocked off the stalks,
then the grains were
stored in a granary.
The corn was poured
in at the top. It was taken
out through a hatch at
the bottom when it was
needed for making bread.

corn in here

out here

If you were a rich Ancient Egyptian you would own a large herd
of cattle. Poor farmers had a few goats, pigs, ducks or geese.

a rich Ancient Egyptian
counting his cattle

a poor Ancient Egyptian
feeding his animals

STAGE 3

Make some bricks

Ancient Egyptian houses were built using bricks made of mud. The mud was pushed into a wooden mould, then tipped out and left in the sun until it was hard.

In the towns the houses were built close to each other with narrow lanes in-between for shade in the hot weather. Some houses were two or three floors high and several families might live in each house.

The roof was used as another room. It was cooler up there.

ventilator on roof to bring cool air into the house

small windows to keep out heat and dust

The walls were covered in mud and painted white to keep them cool.

If you were a rich person, you lived in a big house with many rooms. The walls were painted with patterns and bright colours. There might be a garden outside with a pool and trees.

These houses would have bedrooms, a kitchen and storerooms. In the middle of each house there would be a large room used as a sitting room.

furniture from a rich person's house

lamp→

table

armchair

headrest in the shape of a hare

bed

mattress for bed

cabinet

stool with cushion

storage box

STAGE 4

Bake some bread

If you were an Ancient Egyptian you would have eaten lots of bread. The bread was made in clay pots placed on the fire. Honey or fruit was used to make sweet cakes.

bread pot on a brazier

The Ancient Egyptians did most of their cooking on a brazier. This was a flat pan that held the charcoal. Charcoal is a kind of wood that gets very hot but doesn't make much smoke or many flames. To light the charcoal you had to twirl a wooden stick!

Fish and meat were dried in the hot sun. Then they could be stored and eaten later.

How to light charcoal

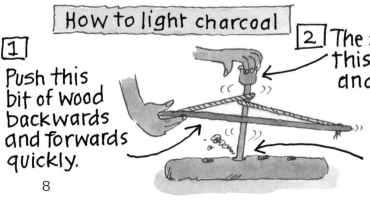

1 Push this bit of wood backwards and forwards quickly.

2 The string twirls this stick round and round.

3 The two bits of wood rub together and get red hot.

If you were a wealthy Ancient Egyptian you could invite friends over for a feast. You could serve roast or boiled beef. There were lots of fruit and vegetables to eat and beer and wine to drink. You drank the beer through a drinking tube – a bit like a straw!

honey

olives

grapes

lettuce

roast duck

sliced onions

figs

cucumber

melon

fish

date jam

bread

Go shopping

Town centres were busy, noisy places. The owners of the market stalls called out to people who were passing. The Ancient Egyptians didn't use money. If you went shopping you had to take something to give away in **exchange**. It might be fish from the river or vegetables you had grown. This was called bartering.

Policemen patrolled the markets to stop shoplifters. Instead of dogs, they had baboons to scare people.

A lot of noise came from the workshops in the town. The Ancient Egyptians liked to make beautiful things. If you were an Ancient Egyptian you might be a **carpenter** or a **weaver**. You might make baskets or pots, fine glass or fancy jewellery.

blowing glass into the shape of a jar in the glass maker's shop

butcher's shop

a fruit seller

basket maker

Wear a wig

If you were an Ancient Egyptian it was easy to get dressed in the morning. Most people wore just a **loincloth** or a simple dress. The clothes were nearly always white to keep them cool.

farm worker
with a leather
loincloth

man with
a pleated
linen loincloth

important man
wearing a linen robe

Women wore
long white
dresses.

see-through
material over
a dress

Boys and girls wore
their hair in ponytails.
Boys had most of
their hair shaved off.

12

Rich Ancient Egyptians shaved their heads and wore wigs. They were made of real hair stuck together with beeswax. Wigs were cleaner and cooler than normal hair.

Sometimes Ancient Egyptians mixed perfume into a lump of animal fat. They wore it like a little hat. The fat melted in the heat and the perfume trickled through the hair – like an air-freshener!

Both men and women wore wide collars of beads or scented flowers.

If you were a rich woman, you spent a lot of time making yourself beautiful.

After your bath, you put on make-up and jewellery.

dark eye make-up →

blusher

big earrings

bead necklace

box of cosmetics →

comb

Serve the king

The king of Ancient Egypt was called the pharaoh. The name means "big house" in Ancient Egyptian because the king lived in a huge palace. The pharaoh was very rich. His furniture was often covered in gold. He and his wife wore expensive clothes.

The pharaoh had three different crowns.

false beard →

Each crown had a badge of the snake goddess at the front. Egyptians believed it spat poison at the pharaoh's enemies.

Only a few women became pharaohs. They had to wear the false beard, too!

The Ancient Egyptian people thought the pharaoh was a god as well as a human. They expected him to protect them at all times. He might use his army to defend them against enemies. He might give grain from the royal store if the people were starving.

Perhaps you were one of the hundreds of people who served the pharaoh in his palace. Perhaps you looked after his horses or gathered flowers for the royal rooms. Perhaps you were the royal fan bearer: you kept the pharaoh cool with a huge fan of ostrich feathers. You might be more important than that – like the keeper of the king's treasure or inspector of buildings. Most important of all was the royal vizier.

royal vizier

The royal vizier was like a **prime minister**. He kept his eyes and ears open. He knew everything that went on. Anyone could come to him with a problem.

I'm having trouble with my neighbour.

I want to report a theft.

There's a mistake in this report about my farm.

Feed a god

If you were an Ancient Egyptian you might have a statue of Bes by your front door. He looked like an ugly little man but he was a friendly god who chased evil spirits away from your home.

Bes rattled a tambourine to scare away poisonous snakes.

The Ancient Egyptians had hundreds of gods. You could choose which ones you wanted to ask for protection or help. You kept little statues of the gods in your house, prayed to them and left food for them to eat.

The Ancient Egyptians thought that some gods lived inside animals. When they made a statue of a god they often gave it the head of an animal.

The god Ra was father of the gods. The Ancient Egyptians thought he carried the sun across the sky every day.

Ra had the head of a falcon. Falcons flew high in the sky and had good eyesight.

Some people wore a little badge shaped like Ra's eye. → The Ancient Egyptians believed it protected them from evil.

You prayed to Bastet, the cat goddess, to give you a good harvest of grain.

Some gods were nasty. Seth was the god of the desert. Ancient Egyptians believed he made sandstorms when he was angry.

17

Enjoy yourself

The Ancient Egyptians built **temples** for the gods to live in.
If you were a priest, you looked after the statue of
the god in the temple. You kept it clean and brought
it food. It might be Amun, the god of the winds, or Ra,
the god of the sun. Once a year the god's statue was
brought out of the temple and priests carried it round
the countryside. This was an excuse
for people to come and watch,
dance and sing.

temple →

The god's statue was carried in a box on a boat.

Shopkeepers set up stalls to sell snacks and souvenirs to the crowds

18

The Ancient Egyptians liked to play board games. One was called "The Snake". The board was shaped like a coiled snake. The player who reached the middle first was the winner.

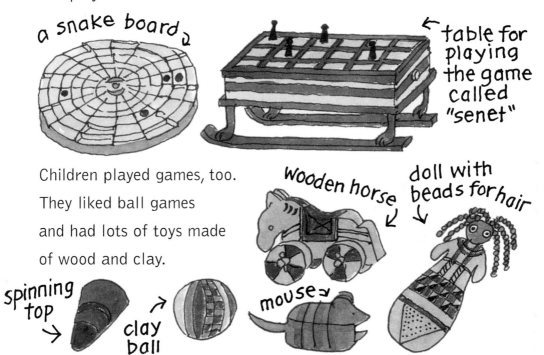

a snake board

← table for playing the game called "senet"

Children played games, too. They liked ball games and had lots of toys made of wood and clay.

wooden horse

doll with beads for hair

spinning top →

clay ball

mouse

All Ancient Egyptians loved to listen to stories — especially scary ones! They liked to laugh, too. Sometimes they painted funny cartoons on their walls.

19

Make a mummy

The Ancient Egyptians believed that when you died, your **spirit** moved on to the next life. However, the spirit often came back to its old body. The body had to be kept ready for the spirit's return. To do this the body was **embalmed** and turned into a mummy.

If you were an Ancient Egyptian who embalmed bodies, you carried out a special **ceremony** every time you made a mummy. The ceremony lasted 70 days.

Stages of the ceremony

1 You used a special tool to pick the brains out through the nostrils!

2 You removed the **organs** from the body and stored them in special jars. →

3 Then you covered the body in a special kind of sand. This had chemicals in it which dried out the body.

20

4 When the body was dry you stuffed it with sawdust, leaves or pads of cloth.

5 You wrapped the body in long strips of cloth.

6 You put the mummy in a coffin. This was usually brightly painted.

7 The last part of the ceremony was called "opening of the mouth".

A priest touched the mouth with a special stick. This allowed the spirit of the dead person to see, hear and move about.

Another priest wore the mask of Anubis. He was the god of death.

STAGE 11

Build a tomb

If you could afford it, you built yourself a tomb. Your body was put in it when you died. It had a false door so your spirit could go out and back in. Other things were put in the tomb — things you might need in the next life. There might be some food and drink or wooden models of things you had in your first life like a boat or your cattle.

finished pyramid →

a new pyramid being built

workers moving the stone

Some pharaohs built themselves enormous tombs, like the pyramids. They took about 20 years to build. Millions of heavy blocks of stone were used. They were pulled into place by gangs of men. The pharaoh's body was laid in the centre of the pyramid and the door was sealed.

Some of the pharaohs and other wealthy people were buried in secret places out in the desert hills. This was to try and stop robbers raiding the tombs for the gold and other treasure that was buried with the mummy.

Heavy blocks of stone are brought by boat.

Make your mark

In Ancient Egypt, scribes were important. They wrote things down for other people. They wrote letters and lists of things that had to be done. They noted down how much **tax** businessmen had to pay and how many cattle farmers owned. They kept records of important events like battles.

If you wanted to be a scribe you had to train for many years.

Scribes wrote on papyrus. This was paper made from a plant called a reed. ← a reed.

The soft inside of the reed was cut into strips. The strips were hammered together to make a smooth surface.

↖ grinder for grinding up soot or earth to make ink

palette ↘

sticks for writing with ↓

24
↳ Ink went in here.

Some scribes wrote on walls.
They used picture writing
called hieroglyphs.

The Ancient Egyptians liked
to cover their buildings with
hieroglyphs and other pictures,
so some scribes became painters.
Students drew the outlines of
the pictures. The chief artists
checked them for mistakes,
then the drawings were painted
in bright colours.

25

Leave something behind

Because Ancient Egypt was a very dry country, things like
mud bricks, wood, paper and even food didn't rot
away quickly. Some of the things the Ancient Egyptians
made and used thousands of years ago have been found.

a piece of a tile

a loaf of bread in a basket

a glove

The paintings on the walls of Ancient Egyptian buildings
give us a picture of what daily life was like in those times.

a workman balances on scaffolding

women playing the flute and harp

The tomb of a pharaoh called Tutankhamun was discovered in 1922. The tomb was filled with the things that the pharaoh might need in his next life – everything from baskets of fruit to fabulous gold statues.

Some of the things found in Tutankhamun's tomb:

wooden couch

carved heads of cows

a box of shawabti, little wooden figures who would become the pharaoh's servants in the next life

a trumpet

model ship

headrest

sandals

pot for face cream

wooden chest

All these things show us just what life was like in Egypt thousands of years ago. Now you know how to be an Ancient Egyptian!

Glossary

canals   wide man-made channels full of water

carpenter   a person who makes things out of wood

ceremony   a special event where actions have to be done
                      in a particular order

cosmetics   creams and powders designed to make people
                      look and smell better

embalmed   treated with special chemicals that stop decay

exchange   a swap

loincloth   a piece of material that you wrapped around
                      your hips and bottom

organs   parts of the body that do special jobs,
                      e.g. the heart, lungs, liver and brain

palette   a flat piece of wood that artists use to hold
                      their paints, ink and brushes while they
                      are working

prime minister   a person who works for a king or queen
                      and who is in charge of running a country

spirit   a person's mind and feelings

tax   the part of a person's earnings that they
                      have to give to the government each year

temples   special buildings where people can
                      worship gods

weaver   a person who makes cloth

Index

The Ancient Egyptians

rich

house   clothes   work

poor

food

burial

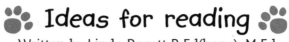

Ideas for reading

Written by Linda Pagett B.Ed(hons), M.Ed
Lecturer and Educational Consultant

Learning objectives: use syntax, context and word structure to build their store of vocabulary as they read for meaning; present information ensuring relevant details are included; use illustrations for different purposes; spell unfamiliar words using grapheme phoneme correspondences; use some drama strategies to explore issues

Curriculum links: History: What can we find out about ancient Egypt from what has survived?

Interest words: canals, embalmed, hieroglyphs, loincloth, papyrus, pharaoh, pyramids, scaffolding, scribes, sickle

Resources: whiteboard, writing materials, world map

Getting started

This book can be read over two or more guided reading sessions.

- Encourage children to find Egypt on a world map and discuss what children already know about the country and people who live there.

- Look at the front cover and blurb together and invite children to speculate what the 13 stages might be, writing down their suggestions on the whiteboard, including any questions they have about Ancient Egyptians that they would like to be answered.

- Turn to the glossary and make sure that children are familiar with any new vocabulary.

Reading and responding

- Read Stage 1 together. Discuss the use of captions and labels and why this is different to the main text. *Do they help readers to understand the artwork?*

- Give children parts in pairs as farmers, builders, bakers, market stall holders, wigmakers or people who serve the king. Using the contents, give them relevant stages 2–7 to read together.

- Hear children report back to the group in role, explaining how, when and why they do their job. Question them for any missing detail, e.g. *could you tell us what you make the wigs from?*